AS I LAY DYING

William Faulkner

TECHNICAL DIRECTOR Maxwell Krohn
EDITORIAL DIRECTOR Justin Kestler
MANAGING EDITOR Ben Florman

SERIES EDITORS Boomie Aglietti, Justin Kestler
PRODUCTION Christian Lorentzen

WRITERS Jim Cocola, Valerie Jaffee
EDITORS Benjamin Morgan, Thomas Connors, Boomie Aglietti

This edition published by Spark Publishing

Spark Publishing
A Division of SparkNotes LLC
120 Fifth Avenue, 8th Floor
New York, NY 10011

02 03 04 05 SN 9 8 7 6 5 4 3 2 1

Please send all comments and questions or report errors to
feedback@sparknotes.com.

Library of Congress information available upon request

Printed and bound in the United States

RRD-C

ISBN 1-58663-399-6

INTRODUCTION: STOPPING TO BUY SPARKNOTES ON A SNOWY EVENING

Whose words these are you *think* you know.
Your paper's due tomorrow, though;
We're glad to see you stopping here
To get some help before you go.

Lost your course? You'll find it here.
Face tests and essays without fear.
Between the words, good grades at stake:
Get great results throughout the year.

Once school bells caused your heart to quake
As teachers circled each mistake.
Use SparkNotes and no longer weep,
Ace every single test you take.

Yes, books are lovely, dark, and deep,
But only what you grasp you keep,
With hours to go before you sleep,
With hours to go before you sleep.

CONTENTS

NOTE: In 1985, noted Faulkner critic Noel Polk corrected the text of *As I Lay Dying* to reflect Faulkner's own ribbon setting copy more closely than previous editions had. This SparkNote refers to Polk's corrected edition, *As I Lay Dying: The Corrected Text*, published by Vintage Books in 1990. For ease of reference, this SparkNote numbers the fifty-nine sections that make up the novel.

CONTEXT

CONTEXT

WILLIAM FAULKNER WAS BORN in New Albany, Mississippi, on September 25, 1897, the oldest of four brothers in a southern family of aristocratic origin. Faulkner spent much of his life in and around his beloved hometown of Oxford, Mississippi, where he worked various odd jobs and wrote in his spare time in the years leading up to his literary fame. Stints in New York and Paris introduced Faulkner to the culture and major figures of the Modernist literary movement, an early twentieth-century response to a world marked by rapid and often bewildering technological development. Modernism in literature was characterized by experimentation with language and literary conventions, and Faulkner became one of the movement's major figures. In 1924, Faulkner published his first book, a collection of poetry titled *The Marble Faun.* Faulkner published his fourth novel, *The Sound and the Fury,* in 1929, and though *The Sound and the Fury* is often considered his masterpiece, it was his sixth novel, *Sanctuary,* in 1929, that finally won him an audience and a literary career. *The Sound and the Fury,* however, marked the beginning of Faulkner's use of experimental narrative techniques to explore the psychological complexity of his characters and their interactions more thoroughly than a traditional style would have allowed.

As I Lay Dying, originally published in 1930, is one of the most vivid testaments to the power of this new style, with Faulkner's usually complex and lengthy paragraphs trimmed down with a conscientious economy to form a clear, unified plot. Much of this clarity can be attributed to the intensity of Faulkner's vision for the work and the careful planning and outlining he did before sitting down to write. Whereas Faulkner conceived many of his other works in a scattered fashion, he fully imagined the innovative concepts of *As I Lay Dying* ahead of time, furiously scribbling down his revelations on the back of an upturned wheelbarrow. This organization reflects the great hopes that Faulkner pinned on the novel—he had recently married his high school sweetheart, Estelle Oldham, and hoped his saga of the Bundren family would finally ensure a steady income for his family and a greater literary reputation for himself. The result is a novel of some daring, one that forgoes the unified perspective of a

I

single narrator and fragments its text into fifty-nine segments voiced from fifteen different perspectives. In writing *As I Lay Dying* in this way, Faulkner requires his readers to take an active part in constructing the story, allows for multiple and sometimes conflicting interpretations, and achieves remarkable levels of psychological insight.

In *As I Lay Dying*, Faulkner first introduces Yoknapatawpha County, a fictional rendition of his native Lafayette County, Mississippi, which became the setting for most of his best-known works. The novels set in Yoknapatawpha County can even be read as one intricate story, in which the same places, events, families, and people turn up over and over again. For example, Vernon and Cora Tull, who appear in *As I Lay Dying*, also appear in *The Hamlet*, a later novel. Before Faulkner, the American South was widely portrayed in American literature as a backward, impossibly foreign land. The complexity and sophistication of the Yoknapatawpha novels changed many of these perceptions, and it is largely due to Faulkner's influence that the South is now recognized as one of the country's most fertile literary regions. Faulkner himself, however, did not fare well financially, and he was eventually forced to take work as a screenwriter in Hollywood to supplement his dwindling income. His fortunes were revived, however, with the 1946 publication of *The Portable Faulkner*, which featured a large and varied selection of his writings. He won the Nobel Prize in Literature in 1949, and a pair of Pulitzer Prizes followed in 1955 and 1962. Faulkner continued to write about Yoknapatawpha until his death in Byhalia, Mississippi, on July 6, 1962, at the age of sixty-four.

PLOT OVERVIEW

ADDIE BUNDREN, THE WIFE of Anse Bundren and the matriarch of a poor southern family, is very ill, and is expected to die soon. Her oldest son, Cash, puts all of his carpentry skills into preparing her coffin, which he builds right in front of Addie's bedroom window. Although Addie's health is failing rapidly, two of her other sons, Darl and Jewel, leave town to make a delivery for the Bundrens' neighbor, Vernon Tull, whose wife and two daughters have been tending to Addie. Shortly after Darl and Jewel leave, Addie dies. The youngest Bundren child, Vardaman, associates his mother's death with that of a fish he caught and cleaned earlier that day. With some help, Cash completes the coffin just before dawn. Vardaman is troubled by the fact that his mother is nailed shut inside a box, and while the others sleep, he bores holes in the lid, two of which go through his mother's face. Addie and Anse's daughter, Dewey Dell, whose recent sexual liaisons with a local farmhand named Lafe have left her pregnant, is so overwhelmed by anxiety over her condition that she barely mourns her mother's death. A funeral service is held on the following day, where the women sing songs inside the Bundren house while the men stand outside on the porch talking to each other.

Darl, who narrates much of this first section, returns with Jewel a few days later, and the presence of buzzards over their house lets them know their mother is dead. On seeing this sign, Darl sardonically reassures Jewel, who is widely perceived as ungrateful and uncaring, that he can be sure his beloved horse is not dead. Addie has made Anse promise that she will be buried in the town of Jefferson, and though this request is a far more complicated proposition than burying her at home, Anse's sense of obligation, combined with his desire to buy a set of false teeth, compels him to fulfill Addie's dying wish. Cash, who has broken his leg on a job site, helps the family lift the unbalanced coffin, but it is Jewel who ends up manhandling it, almost single-handedly, into the wagon. Jewel refuses, however, to actually come in the wagon, and follows the rest of the family riding on his horse, which he bought when he was young by secretly working nights on a neighbor's land.

On the first night of their journey, the Bundrens stay at the home of a generous local family, who regards the Bundrens' mission with skepticism. Due to severe flooding, the main bridges leading over the local river have been flooded or washed away, and the Bundrens are forced to turn around and attempt a river-crossing over a makeshift ford. When a stray log upsets the wagon, the coffin is knocked out, Cash's broken leg is reinjured, and the team of mules drowns. Vernon Tull sees the wreck, and helps Jewel rescue the coffin and the wagon from the river. Together, the family members and Tull search the riverbed for Cash's tools.

Cora, Tull's wife, remembers Addie's unchristian inclination to respect her son Jewel more than God. Addie herself, speaking either from her coffin or in a leap back in time to her deathbed, recalls events from her life: her loveless marriage to Anse; her affair with the local minister, Whitfield, which led to Jewel's conception; and the birth of her various children. Whitfield recalls traveling to the Bundrens' house to confess the affair to Anse, and his eventual decision not to say anything after all.

A horse doctor sets Cash's broken leg, while Cash faints from the pain without ever complaining. Anse is able to purchase a new team of mules by mortgaging his farm equipment, using money that he was saving for his false teeth and money that Cash was saving for a new gramophone, and trading in Jewel's horse. The family continues on its way. In the town of Mottson, residents react with horror to the stench coming from the Bundren wagon. While the family is in town, Dewey Dell tries to buy a drug that will abort her unwanted pregnancy, but the pharmacist refuses to sell it to her, and advises marriage instead. With cement the family has purchased in town, Darl creates a makeshift cast for Cash's broken leg, which fits poorly and only increases Cash's pain. The Bundrens then spend the night at a local farm owned by a man named Gillespie. Darl, who has been skeptical of their mission for some time, burns down the Gillespie barn with the intention of incinerating the coffin and Addie's rotting corpse. Jewel rescues the animals in the barn, then risks his life to drag out Addie's coffin. Darl lies on his mother's coffin and cries.

The next day, the Bundrens arrive in Jefferson and bury Addie. Rather than face a lawsuit for Darl's criminal barn burning, the Bundrens claim that Darl is insane, and give him to a pair of men who commit him to a Jackson mental institution. Dewey Dell tries again to buy an abortion drug at the local pharmacy, where a boy working behind the counter claims to be a doctor and tricks her into exchanging sexual services for what she soon realizes is not an actual abor-

tion drug. The following morning, the children are greeted by their father, who sports a new set of false teeth and, with a mixture of shame and pride, introduces them to his new bride, a local woman he meets while borrowing shovels with which to bury Addie.

CHARACTER LIST

Addie Bundren The wife of Anse Bundren and mother to Cash, Darl, Jewel, Dewey Dell, and Vardaman. Addie is a mostly absent protagonist, and her death triggers the novel's action. She is a former schoolteacher whose bitter, loveless life causes her to despise her husband and to invest all of her love in her favorite child, Jewel, rather than in the rest of her family or God.

Anse Bundren The head of the Bundren family. Anse is a poor farmer afflicted with a hunchback, whose instincts are overwhelmingly selfish. His poor childrearing skills seem to be largely responsible for his children's various predicaments. Alternately hated and disrespected by his children, Anse nonetheless succeeds in achieving his two greatest goals in one fell swoop: burying his dead wife in her hometown of Jefferson, and acquiring a new set of false teeth.

Darl Bundren The second Bundren child. Darl is the most sensitive and articulate of the surviving Bundrens and delivers the greatest number of interior monologues in the novel. As the family encounters disaster upon disaster during the trip, Darl's frustration with the whole process leads him to try to end things decisively by incinerating his dead mother's coffin.

Jewel The bastard child of Addie and Whitfield, the minister. Though Darl seems to understand him, Jewel remains the novel's greatest mystery, and is the least represented in its many sections. Jewel has a proud, fiercely independent nature that most of his family and neighbors confuse for selfishness. His passionate, brooding nature, however, reveals a real love and dedication to his mother, and he becomes a fierce protector of her coffin.

Cash Bundren The eldest Bundren child and a skilled carpenter. Cash is the paragon of patience and selflessness, almost to the point of absurdity. He refuses ever to complain about his broken, festering leg, allowing the injury to degenerate to the point that he may never walk again. Cash emerges as one of the novel's few consistently stable characters.

Dewey Dell Bundren The only Bundren daughter. Dewey Dell is seventeen, and a recent sexual experience has left her pregnant. Increasingly desperate, she finds her mind occupied exclusively with her pregnancy, and views all men with varying degrees of suspicion.

Vardaman Bundren The youngest of the Bundren children. Vardaman has a lively imagination, and he views his mother's death through the same lens with which he views a fish he has recently caught and cleaned. Although his ramblings at the beginning of the novel border on the maniacal, Vardaman proves to be a thoughtful and innocent child.

Vernon Tull The Bundrens' wealthier neighbor. Tull is both a critic of and an unappreciated help to the Bundrens. He hires Darl, Jewel, and Cash for odd jobs, and helps the family cross the river in spite of its overt hostility toward him. Tull and his wife Cora, however, are critical of the Bundrens' decision to bury Addie's body in Jefferson.

Cora Tull Vernon Tull's wife. Cora stays with Addie during Addie's final hours. A deeply religious woman and pious to a fault, Cora frequently and vocally disapproves of Addie's impiety and behavior.

Lafe The father of Dewey Dell's child. While he never appears in person in the novel, Lafe is certainly a driving force behind many of Dewey Dell's thoughts and much of her behavior. In a supreme effort to disassociate himself from her problems, Lafe gives Dewey Dell ten dollars with which to pay for an abortion.

Whitfield The local minister. Held up by Cora Tull as the pinnacle of piety, Whitfield is in fact a hypocrite. His affair with Addie results in Jewel's conception, and, though Whitfield resolves to confess the affair to Anse, he ends up deciding that the mere intention to confess will do just as well.

Peabody The severely overweight rural doctor who attends to Addie and later to Cash. Peabody is extremely critical of the way Anse treats his children.

Samson The local farmer who puts up the Bundrens on the first evening of their disastrous funeral journey. Samson sees the Bundrens' problems as a judgment on the family's uncouth manners and on Addie and Anse's disregard for God and their own children.

Armstid A local farmer who puts up the Bundrens on the second evening of their funeral journey. Anse repeatedly and rigidly refuses Armstid's offer to lend Anse a team of mules.

Gillespie A farmer who puts up the Bundrens later in their journey.

Moseley The Mottson druggist who indignantly refuses Dewey Dell's request for an abortion. Moseley's stern lecture to Dewey Dell is both the embodiment of sanctimoniousness and, some might say, of fatherly caring.

CHARACTER LIST

MacGowan A rather despicable young employee at a Jefferson drugstore. MacGowan extorts a sexual favor from Dewey Dell in return for a fake abortion treatment.

The Gillespie boy Gillespie's son, who helps Jewel save the animals from the burning barn.

ANALYSIS OF MAJOR CHARACTERS

ADDIE BUNDREN

Though she is dead for most of the novel, Addie is one of its most important characters, as her unorthodox wish to be buried near her blood relatives rather than with her own family is at the core of the story. Addie, whose voice is expressed through Cora Tull's memories and through her own brief section in the narrative, appears to be a strong-willed and intelligent woman haunted by a sense of disillusionment. Unable to bring herself to love the coarse, helpless Anse or the children she bears him, Addie sees marital love and motherhood as empty concepts, words that exist solely to fill voids in people's lives. After she bears a second child to Anse, Addie first expresses her wish to be buried far away, stating her belief that "the reason for living [is] to get ready to stay dead a long time." The little value she does find in life, from her brief affair with Whitfield and her love for her son Jewel, ends on a morbid note. Jewel treats Addie harshly while she is alive, and only once she is dead does he "save [her] from the water and from the fire," as she always believed he would. Addie invests her life and energy in a love that finds repayment and comes to fruition only after she is dead.

As a corpse, Addie is equally important to the novel, hindering and dividing her family as much as when she is alive. Many of the incidents after Addie's death reflect this feeling that some part of Addie is still living. Vardaman drills holes in the coffin so that the dead Addie might have air to breathe, and when Darl and Vardaman listen to the noises of the decomposing body, Darl claims that these sounds are Addie speaking. Even the stench of Addie's corpse captivates a large audience of strangers. The notion that there is continuity between the articulate human voice of the living Addie and the putrid biological mass that is the dead Addie is among the most emotionally powerful ideas presented in the novel.

DARL BUNDREN

Darl, who speaks in nineteen of the novel's fifty-nine sections, is in many ways its most cerebral character. Darl's knack for probing analysis and poetic descriptions mean that his voice becomes the closest thing the story offers to a guiding, subjective narrator. Yet it is this same intellectual nature that prevents him from achieving either the flashy heroism of his brother Jewel or the self-sacrificing loyalty of his brother Cash. In fact, it prevents Darl from believing wholeheartedly in the family's mission. Darl registers his objection to the entire burial outing by apparently abandoning his mother's coffin during the botched river-crossing, and by setting fire to Gillespie's barn with the eight-day-old corpse inside.

Another consequence of Darl's philosophical nature is his alienation from the community around him. According to Cora Tull, people find Darl strange and unsettling. He is also able to understand private things about the lives of the people around him, as he does when he guesses at Dewey Dell's fling with Lafe or perceives that Anse is not Jewel's real father. At times, Darl is almost clairvoyant, as evidenced by the scene in which he is able to describe vividly the scene at his mother's death, even though he and Jewel are far away from the scene when she dies. Other characters alienate Darl for fear that he will get too close to them and their secrets. It is perhaps this fear, more than Darl's act of arson, that leads his family to have him committed to an insane asylum at the end of the novel—after all, Dewey Dell, who realizes that Darl knows her sordid secret, is the first to restrain him when the officers from the asylum arrive.

JEWEL BUNDREN

Because Jewel speaks very few words of his own throughout the novel, he is defined by his actions, as filtered through the eyes of other characters. Jewel's uncommunicative nature creates a great distance between him and us, and a great deal of room exists for debating the meaning of Jewel's actions. Darl's frequent descriptions of Jewel as "wooden" reinforce the image of Jewel as impenetrable to others, and also establish a relationship between Jewel and the wooden coffin that comes to symbolize his mother. Whether or not Jewel returns his mother's devotion is also debatable—his behavior toward her while she is alive seems callous. Even as Addie lies on her deathbed, Jewel refuses to say good-bye to her, and harshly asserts his independence from her earlier on with his purchase of a horse. Jewel's actions after Addie's death show, however, that Jewel does care deeply about her, as he makes great sacrifices to assure the safe passage of her body to her chosen resting place, agreeing even to the sale of his beloved horse. Similarly, Jewel's cold, rough-spoken behavior toward the rest of his family contrasts sharply with the heroic devotion he demonstrates in his deeds, such as when he searches valiantly for Cash's tools after the river-crossing and nearly comes to blows with a stranger whom he believes has insulted the family. In general, Jewel is an independent, solitary man of action, and these traits put him in an antagonistic relationship with the introspective Darl.

CHARACTER ANALYSIS

THEMES, MOTIFS & SYMBOLS

THEMES

Themes are the fundamental and often universal ideas explored in a literary work.

THE IMPERMANENCE OF EXISTENCE AND IDENTITY

The death of Addie Bundren inspires several characters to wrestle with the rather sizable questions of existence and identity. Vardaman is bewildered and horrified by the transformation of a fish he caught and cleaned into "pieces of not-fish," and associates that image with the transformation of Addie from a person into an indefinable nonperson. Jewel never really speaks for himself, but his grief is summed up for him by Darl, who says that Jewel's mother is a horse. For his own part, Darl believes that since the dead Addie is now best described as "was" rather than "is," it must be the case that she no longer exists. If his mother does not exist, Darl reasons, then Darl has no mother and, by implication, does not exist. These speculations are not mere games of language and logic. Rather, they have tangible, even terrible, consequences for the novel's characters. Vardaman and Darl, the characters for whom these questions are the most urgent, both find their hold on reality loosened as they pose such inquiries. Vardaman babbles senselessly early in the novel, while Darl is eventually declared insane. The fragility and uncertainty of human existence is further illustrated at the end of the novel, when Anse introduces his new wife as "Mrs. Bundren," a name that, until recently, has belonged to Addie. If the identity of Mrs. Bundren can be usurped so quickly, the inevitable conclusion is that any individual's identity is equally unstable.

THE TENSION BETWEEN WORDS AND THOUGHTS

Addie's assertion that words are "just words," perpetually falling short of the ideas and emotions they seek to convey, reflects the distrust with which the novel as a whole treats verbal communication. While the inner monologues that make up the novel demonstrate that the characters have rich inner lives, very little of the content of these inner lives is ever communicated between individuals. Indeed, conversations tend to be terse, halting, and irrelevant to what the characters are thinking at the time. When, for example, Tull and several other local men are talking with Cash about his broken leg during Addie's funeral, we are presented with two entirely separate conversations. One, printed in normal type, is vague and simple and is presumably the conversation that is actually occurring. The second, in italics, is far richer in content and is presumably the one that the characters would have if they actually spoke their minds. All of the characters are so fiercely protective of their inner thoughts that the rich content of their minds is translated to only the barest, most begrudging scraps of dialogue, which in turn leads to any number of misunderstandings and miscommunications.

THE RELATIONSHIP BETWEEN
CHILDBEARING AND DEATH

As I Lay Dying is, in its own way, a relentlessly cynical novel, and it robs even childbirth of its usual rehabilitative powers. Instead of functioning as an antidote to death, childbirth seems an introduction to it—for both Addie and Dewey Dell, giving birth is a phenomenon that kills the people closest to it, even if they are still physically alive. For Addie, the birth of her first child seems like a cruel trick, an infringement on her precious solitude, and it is Cash's birth that first causes Addie to refer to Anse as dead. Birth becomes for Addie a final obligation, and she sees both Dewey Dell and Vardaman as reparations for the affair that led to Jewel's conception, the last debts she must pay before preparing herself for death. Dewey Dell's feelings about pregnancy are no more positive: her condition becomes a constant concern, causes her to view all men as potential sexual predators, and transforms her entire world, as she says in an early section, into a "tub full of guts." Birth seems to spell out a prescribed death for women and, by proxy, the metaphorical deaths of their entire households.

MOTIFS

Motifs are recurring structures, contrasts, or literary devices that can help to develop and inform the text's major themes.

POINTLESS ACTS OF HEROISM

As I Lay Dying is filled with moments of great heroism and with struggles that are almost epic, but the novel's take on such battles is ironic at best, and at times it even makes them seem downright absurd or mundane. The Bundrens' effort to get their wagon across the flooded river is a struggle that could have been pulled from a more conventional adventure novel, but is undermined by the fact that it occurs for a questionable purpose. One can argue that the mission of burying Addie in Jefferson is as much about Anse's false teeth as about Addie's dying wishes. Cash's martyrdom seems noble, but his uncomplaining tolerance of the pain from his injuries eventually becomes more ridiculous than heroic. Jewel's rescuing of the livestock is daring, but it also nullifies Darl's burning of the barn, which, while criminal, could be seen as the most daring and noble act of all. Every act of heroism, if not ridiculous on its own, counteracts an equally epic act, a vicious cycle that lends an absurdity that is both comic and tragic to the novel.

INTERIOR MONOLOGUES

As Faulkner was embarking on his literary career in the early twentieth century, a number of Modernist writers were experimenting with narrative techniques that depended more on explorations of individual consciousness than on a string of events to create a story. James Joyce's *Ulysses* and Marcel Proust's *In Search of Lost Time* are among the most famous and successful of these experiments, but Faulkner also made a substantial contribution to this movement.

As I Lay Dying is written as a series of stream-of-consciousness monologues, in which the characters' thoughts are presented in all their uncensored chaos, without the organizing presence of an objective narrator. This technique turns character psychology into a dominant concern and is able to present that psychology with much more complexity and authority than a more traditional narrative style. At the same time, it forces us to work hard to understand the text. Instead of being presented with an objective framework of events, somewhere in the jumble of images, memories, and unexplained allusions, we are forced to take the pieces each character gives and make something of them ourselves.

Issues of Social Class

In the American South, where Faulkner lived and wrote, social class was more hierarchical and loomed larger as a concern than elsewhere in the United States, and it is clearly engrained in the fabric of *As I Lay Dying.* Faulkner proved to be unusual in his ability to depict poor rural folk with grace, dignity, and poetic grandeur, without whitewashing or ignoring their circumstances. The Bundrens find willing, even gracious hosts at neighboring rural farms, but their welcome in the more affluent towns is cold at best: a marshal tells them their corpse smells too rancid for them to stay, a town man pulls a knife on Jewel, and an unscrupulous shop attendant takes advantage of Dewey Dell. On the other hand, despite their poor grammar and limited vocabularies, Faulkner's characters express their thoughts with a sort of pared-down poeticism. Exactly what Faulkner's intentions were for his family of rural southerners is unclear—*As I Lay Dying* has been read as both a poignant tribute to and a scathing send-up of rural southern values—but the Bundrens' background unmistakably shapes their journey and the interactions they have along the way.

SYMBOLS

Symbols are objects, characters, figures, or colors used to represent abstract ideas or concepts.

Animals

Shortly after Addie's death, the Bundren children seize on animals as symbols of their deceased mother. Vardaman declares that his mother is the fish he caught. Darl asserts that Jewel's mother is his horse. Dewey Dell calls the family cow a woman as she mulls over her pregnancy only minutes after she has lost Addie, her only female relative. For very different reasons, the grief-stricken characters seize on animals as emblems of their own situations. Vardaman sees Addie in his fish because, like the fish, she has been transformed to a different state than when she was alive. The cow, swollen with milk, signifies to Dewey Dell the unpleasantness of being stuck with an unwanted burden. Jewel and his horse add a new wrinkle to the use of animals as symbols. To us, based on Darl's word, the horse is a symbol of Jewel's love for his mother. For Jewel, however, the horse, based on his riding of it, apparently symbolizes a hard-won freedom from the Bundren family. That we can draw such different conclusions from the novel's characters makes the horse in many ways representative of the unpredictable and subjective nature of symbols in *As I Lay Dying*.

ADDIE'S COFFIN

Addie's coffin comes to stand literally for the enormous burden of dysfunction that Addie's death, and circumstances in general, place on the Bundren family. Cash, always calm and levelheaded, manufactures the coffin with great craft and care, but the absurdities pile up almost immediately—Addie is placed in the coffin upside down, and Vardaman drills holes in her face. Like the Bundrens' lives, the coffin is thrown off balance by Addie's corpse. The coffin becomes the gathering point for all of the family's dysfunction, and putting it to rest is also crucial to the family's ability to return to some sort of normalcy.

TOOLS

Tools, in the form of Cash's carpentry tools and Anse's farm equipment, become symbols of respectable living and stability thrown into jeopardy by the recklessness of the Bundrens' journey. Cash's tools seem as though they should have significance for Cash alone, but when these tools are scattered by the rushing river and the oncoming log, the whole family, as well as Tull, scrambles to recover them. Anse's farm equipment is barely mentioned, but ends up playing a crucial role in the Bundrens' journey when Anse mortgages the most expensive parts of it to buy a new team of mules. This trade is significant, as the money from Anse's pilfering of Cash's gramophone fund and the sale of Jewel's horse represents the sacrifice of these characters' greatest dreams. But the fact that Anse throws in his farm equipment should not be overlooked, as this equipment guarantees the family's livelihood. In an effort to salvage the burial trip, Anse jeopardizes the very tools the family requires to till its land and survive.

Summary & Analysis

Sections 1–6

From Darl and Jewel's arrival at home to Darl's departure

Darl

Darl Bundren describes walking with his brother Jewel across a field toward their house. They pass a dilapidated cotton house, which Darl walks around but Jewel walks straight through, entering and leaving through the building's large, open windows. They then reach the foot of a bluff, where Vernon Tull, the Bundrens' wealthier neighbor, has stacked two chairs on his wagon. At the top of the bluff, Darl and Jewel's older brother, Cash, is dutifully fitting boards together for a coffin for their mother, Addie. Darl walks past Cash and enters the house.

Cora

The narrative perspective shifts to that of Tull's wife, Cora, who is thinking about some cakes that she was recently hired to make, only to see the order cancelled after she had baked them. Cora's daughter, Kate, rails against the injustice of this turn of events, while Cora takes it in stride. Addie lies nearby, frail and silent, hardly breathing, as Cora's other daughter, Eula, watches over her. Outside, the sound of Cash's sawing continues. Cora recalls Addie's talent for baking cakes. Addie appears to be either asleep or watching Cash's efforts through the window. Darl passes through the hall without a word and heads for the back of the house.

Darl

Darl encounters his father, Anse, and their neighbor, Vernon Tull, sitting on the back porch. Anse asks after Jewel. Darl takes a drink of water, thinking about what a simple pleasure it is to do so, and remembers sneaking out at night to drink water as a child. Darl answers Anse's question, informing his father that Jewel is attending to the horses. In the barn, Jewel struggles violently to mount a horse, before finally leaping onto its back and riding it down and up a hill. When he gets back to the barn, Jewel dismounts and feeds the horse.

JEWEL

Jewel thinks with bitterness and resentment about Cash's insistence on constructing Addie's coffin right outside her window. He is angry with the other members of his family for allowing Cash to proceed in this way. He expresses a wish to be alone with his mother in her final days.

DARL

Darl talks about how he and Jewel are making preparations for a delivery trip they are running for Tull, who is going to pay them three dollars. Anse is hesitant to let them go, as he is worried that Addie will die before Darl and Jewel return with the team of horses. Tull reassures them about Addie, and Jewel lashes out at him for his intrusiveness. Jewel then proceeds to voice his anger toward Cash and the rest of the family for their seeming eagerness to hurry Addie to her end. Anse responds by applauding the family's fortitude in following Addie's last wishes. Finally, Anse agrees to let the boys make the trip, on the condition that they return by the next day at sundown. As Darl enters the house, he reflects on how voices travel in the hallway: "they sound as though they were speaking out of the air about your head."

CORA

Cora watches Darl enter the house and is touched by the emotion with which he bids Addie farewell. She contrasts Darl's sweetness with Anse's and Jewel's callousness. As Darl stands in the doorway, Dewey Dell, his sister, asks him what he wants. He ignores her and instead stares at his mother, "his heart too full for words."

ANALYSIS

As I Lay Dying has no fixed narrator, and is instead composed of a number of different protagonists' successive interior monologues, the rendition of a character's inner thoughts and feelings. Each voice is subjective, shaped by the particular character's views and perceptions, but also makes factual observations about events, moving the story along in a staggered but continuous narrative. While some characters, particularly Darl, narrate in a straightforward, storytelling fashion, others, such as Cora and Jewel, express their thoughts in a confused and contradictory jumble. We have none of the simple comfort of an entirely objective narrator who can reveal the truth—when the various voices present the same character or event in different lights, we have to make decisions about which voice to trust. Faulkner's approach is challenging, but by employing a narrative in which events are described, judged, and interpreted from several different perspectives, he is able to probe his characters' minds deeply. We are not passive observers of dialogue and events; rather, we experience the characters as they experience themselves. When Darl encounters Anse and Tull on the porch, for example, an eternity of thought passes in Darl's mind during the pause between his father's mundane question about Jewel's whereabouts and Darl's equally mundane reply. In Faulkner's world, what a character thinks is frequently more relevant to the story than what a character says.

Faulkner helps us get a grasp on his characters by associating them with objects: before we meet Tull, we encounter his wagon; before we hear Cash speak, we hear the roar of his saw and the chucking of his adze, a cutting tool used for shaping wood; and, of course, before we meet Addie, we see her coffin being assembled. These objects come to stand for the individuals themselves, as symbols of, and clues to, their respective identities. Tull's wagon implies that he is a man of wealth and industry, Cash's saw and adze signify that he is a skilled craftsman, and Addie's coffin signals that her primary role in the novel is played out in her death. We also learn from what the characters do not say. When Darl comes upon Cash, they exchange no words, leaving us to ponder the dull chops of the axe. This tendency toward mute interaction, which is certainly not limited to Darl and Cash, demonstrates how thoroughly the characters in *As I Lay Dying* are cut off from each other. Again, the use of multiple points of view underscores this separation, with the characters so isolated from each other that even their thoughts cannot be mixed.

Faulkner appears to make a sly reference to his own narrative technique with Darl's reflection on the voices "out of the air about your head." While this comment refers specifically to the sound of many voices mixing in the hallway, we can also read Darl's words as an indirect reference by Faulkner to the mosaic of individual voices that constitutes *As I Lay Dying*. When Darl's reflection ends, for example, Cora's monologue begins, describing Darl's good-bye to Addie as "the sweetest thing I ever saw." The tone of these two characters' perspectives is quite different, but the second picks up seamlessly where the first ends. These fluid transitions from one passage to the next allow the story's narrative to progress rather than become inextricably mired in the same incident.

SECTIONS 7–12

From Dewey Dell's memory of Lafe to Addie's death

> *That's what they mean by the love that passeth*
> *understanding: that pride, that furious desire to hide*
> *that abject nakedness which we bring here with us....*
> (See QUOTATIONS, p. 49)

DEWEY DELL

Dewey Dell remembers a time when she went harvesting with Lafe, a worker on the Bundren farm. She had been heading toward the woods with him, but was nervous. Finally, however, they slept together because Dewey Dell "could not help it." Dewey Dell later realized that Darl somehow found out about her and Lafe. She remembers all of these details as Darl stands in the doorway saying good-bye to Addie. Darl tells Dewey Dell that Addie is going to die before he and Jewel return, but that he is taking Jewel anyway because he needs help loading the wagon.

TULL

Tull tries to relieve Anse of his lingering reservations about Darl making the trip. Vardaman, Darl's youngest brother, appears, climbing up the hill with a large fish that he is planning to show to Addie. Anse, unimpressed, orders him to clean the fish before taking it inside. Cora and Tull depart for the evening, as Anse stands dumbly in the room with Addie. Once in the wagon, Cora and Tull speak pessimistically with Kate and Eula about the Bundren situation and the future of the Bundren children.

ANSE

Anse, in his crude, unschooled diction, begins complaining about the weather, his sons, and the commotion of the road. He is convinced that the road that was put in near his house has brought bad luck, and he blames it for Addie's ill health. Vardaman reappears, covered with blood after cleaning his fish. Anse tells Vardaman to go wash his hands. Anse then reflects that he cannot seem to feel much about anything, and blames this lack of sentiment on the weather.

Darl

Meanwhile, Darl is in the wagon with Jewel. He recalls confronting Dewey Dell about her encounter with Lafe. The sun is about to set. Darl voices his belief in the inevitability of Addie's death over and over to Jewel, who remains silent.

Peabody

Addie's doctor, Peabody, makes his way to the Bundren place after being called for by Anse. Peabody notices that a storm is coming. He is very overweight, and needs help climbing the bluff to the Bundren house. After a struggle, he arrives at the family's house. He enters Addie's room and finds Addie perfectly still except for the movement of her eyes. Outside, Peabody asks Anse why he didn't send for a doctor sooner. Dewey Dell interrupts their conversation and they return to Addie's room. Dewey Dell tells Peabody that Addie wants him to leave. Cash continues to saw away, and Addie calls out his name loudly.

Darl

Darl, still on his journey with Jewel, somehow knows what is happening back at the Bundren household. The rest of the family surrounds Addie's bedside. Addie calls out again to Cash, who begins pantomiming the act of putting the coffin pieces together so she can see how they will fit. Dewey Dell flings herself upon Addie, clutching her tightly. Vardaman and Anse look on in silence. At this moment, Addie dies. Dewey Dell calls for her mother, and the narrative flashes over to Jewel and Darl. Darl says Jewel's name twice. Back at the Bundren home, Cash enters the room and Anse gives him the news, telling him that he needs to finish up the coffin quickly. Cash stares at Addie for a time, and then returns to work. Anse tells Dewey Dell that she should prepare supper, and Dewey Dell leaves the room. Anse stands over his dead wife's body and strokes her face awkwardly before returning to the business of the day. The narrative reverts to Darl, who tells Jewel that Addie is dead.

Analysis

With the introduction of several new voices, the narrative becomes more complex and stylized, and we begin to see identical events through the voices of various characters. Because Darl appears so frequently as a narrator, and because his voice has the fewest peculiarities, his story begins to overpower those of the other narrators. Indeed, Darl's mode of speech deviates the least from Faulkner's prose style in other novels, and it is tempting to consider Darl's point of view to be Faulkner's. Further supporting this suggestion, Darl is chosen to narrate Addie's death even though he is not present when it happens. Exactly how Darl knows what is going on back at the house remains a mystery, but his omniscience does put the role of narrator on his shoulders, at least temporarily.

Nonetheless, *As I Lay Dying* relies most heavily on what its characters say, and how they express themselves, to explain their thoughts and motivations. We do not need Darl, or a narrator, to explain that Anse is selfish—this observation is made obvious by the fact that Anse views his wife's death as merely another example of his rotten luck. Anse's colloquial diction tells us that he is rural and uneducated, which gives us a sufficient idea of his background. Furthermore, we can compare disparate voices, like the frantic thoughts of Dewey Dell and the calm reflectiveness of Tull, to get a sense of how these characters differ from one another; Dewey Dell is trapped by her problems, for example, while Tull is so removed that he barely cares.

Ironically, there is an inverse relationship between a character's physical distance from the dying Addie and that character's emotional attachment to Addie. Darl and Jewel, the two characters who care about Addie the most, are far from her when she dies, while those who are preoccupied with other, relatively unimportant matters stand clustered around her deathbed. Anse, for example, is rather flagrantly absorbed in his own concerns at the moment of tragedy. "God's will be done. . . . Now I can get them teeth," Anse says, thinking only of his long-standing desire for false teeth. Dewey Dell throws herself onto Addie's deathbed with unexpected fury, but she seems more interested in her role as her mother's nurse, and her mind is still primarily occupied by her growing problems with Lafe. Darl and Jewel are more thoroughly and constantly preoccupied with the actual loss of their mother than the other characters are. While the two brothers are far from Addie when she dies, Darl's mysterious knowledge of her death arguably demonstrates that they are the most affected by the event.

Jewel's behavior and feelings toward his mother are particularly complex and puzzling. From Cora's point of view, Jewel is an insensitive, spoiled child who displays no qualms about leaving his dying mother. Indeed, although he appears to be Addie's favorite child,

Jewel, unlike Darl, does not even say good-bye to his mother before he leaves. Still, Jewel clearly cares about Addie, and grows deeply indignant at what he considers to be the Tulls' intrusive presence in the household and the insensitivity of Cash's working on Addie's coffin right beneath her window while she is still alive. Moreover, in his interior monologue in the first part of the novel, Jewel expresses a forceful wish to be alone with Addie as she dies. Faulkner is not attempting to emphasize one view of Jewel over another. The difficulty in pinning Jewel down to a single perspective demonstrates the multifaceted nature of his character.

SECTIONS 13–19

From Vardaman's accusation of Peabody to Vardaman's statement that his mother is a fish

VARDAMAN

Vardaman runs out of the house and begins to cry. He sees the spot on the ground where he first laid the fish he caught, and thinks about how the fish is now chopped up into little pieces of "not-fish" and "not-blood." Vardaman reasons that Peabody is responsible for Addie's death and curses him for it. He jumps off the porch and runs into the barn. Still crying, Vardaman picks up a stick and begins beating Peabody's horses, cursing them and blaming them for Addie's death, until they run off. He shoos away a cow that wants milking, and returns to the barn to cry quietly. Cash passes by and Dewey Dell calls out, but Vardaman continues to cry in the dark.

DEWEY DELL

Dewey Dell is again thinking of her union with Lafe and of the pregnancy that has resulted. She thinks, with some bitterness, of how much Peabody could do for her, if only he would. Outside, Cash continues sawing the wood to make Addie's coffin. Dewey Dell begins to prepare a supper of greens and bread, but does not have time to cook the fish that Vardaman has caught. Cash enters the kitchen, announcing that Peabody's team of horses has gotten loose. Anse, Cash, and Peabody begin eating. They invite Dewey Dell to eat with him, but she leaves to look for Vardaman, who is missing. Dewey Dell runs up to the barn, where the cow needs to be milked, but she tells it to wait. Dewey Dell walks among the stalls, repeating Lafe's name to herself. She finds Vardaman hiding in a stall and accuses him of trying to spy on her. Dewey Dell shakes Vardaman violently before sending him away, then returns to her thoughts of Peabody, and how he may be able to help her.

VARDAMAN

Vardaman stares at the coffin. He is disturbed by the thought that Addie is going to be nailed shut inside of it.

TULL

Tull remembers how he and Cora found out Addie was dead when Peabody's team of horses showed up at his door. It is raining when Tull goes to sleep, and the storm is getting worse when he is woken up by a knock at the door. He finds Vardaman there, soaking wet and covered in mud. Vardaman talks incoherently of the fish that he caught earlier. Tull goes out to harness the team, and returns to find Cora and Vardaman sitting in the kitchen. Vardaman is still speaking about his fish. Cora, Tull, and Vardaman make the journey back to the Bundren house, and Tull helps Cash finish building the coffin. Just before daybreak, they place Addie in the coffin and nail it shut. The next morning, they find the coffin bored full of holes and Vardaman asleep next to it. Inadvertently, Vardaman has bored two of the holes through his mother's face. Throughout the chapter, Tull notes that Vardaman's inexplicable behavior is God's judgment upon Anse's failures as a father and husband. At dawn, Cora and Tull return home.

DARL

Darl, still away on the delivery with Jewel, is able to see what is happening far away at his home. He sees Cash and Anse working to complete the coffin. It begins to rain. Cash, though soaked, continues working. Cora and Tull arrive. Cash sends Anse away, and Cash and Tull make a push to complete the coffin. Just before dawn, Cash finally finishes his task. Anse, Cash, Peabody, and Tull carry the coffin inside. As Darl watches this scene, he reflects that he does not know whether he "is" or not, whereas Jewel knows that he "is" because he does not question his own existence.

CASH

Cash very precisely lists the logic behind his decision to make the coffin on a bevel, or a slight slant.

VARDAMAN

Vardaman states that his mother is a fish.

ANALYSIS

The Bundren siblings' varied responses to Addie's death provide us with deeper insight into their characters. Cash's dry, technical list of his reasons for choosing to make the coffin on a bevel could be read as callousness, but one could also argue that his assembly of the coffin in front of Addie's window is a gesture of some kind. Jewel, on the other hand, remains completely uncommunicative in this section, and remains so throughout the novel, as he is the only Bundren child whose narrative is cut off following Addie's death. Dewey Dell speaks frequently, but she is lost in thought over her pregnancy, which not only eclipses her awareness of her mother's death but even manages to distract her during the relatively simple task of finding Vardaman in the barn. Dewey Dell mentions that she laments this inability to focus on Addie's passing, but feels powerless to change it, noting that she cannot think long enough to worry about anything. Dewey Dell's ability to communicate with the cow introduces an affinity for animals that endures throughout the novel. Like the cow in need of milking, Dewey Dell is preoccupied with her own immediate concerns and is unable to contemplate fully matters that are not her own.

While the first sections of the novel make it clear that Darl's voice is the most authoritative, Vardaman's narration takes on increasing importance as the story progresses. Both Darl's and Vardaman's voices find common ground on the incredibly intricate issue of existence. Darl has the air of an amateur philosopher when he ruminates, "I dont know what I am. I dont know if I am or not." For Darl, his mother's transformation from a living person into a thing to be placed in a box brings up the question of what it means to exist. Vardaman wrestles with similar questions, although his thoughts are conducted with the imagination of a child. As he comes to grips with the initial pain of his mother's death, Vardaman observes that there exists "an *is* different from my *is*." Vardaman's endless rants about the fish puzzle the other characters, but they are simply his way of expressing and making sense of his mother's death. Vardaman equates the transformation of a live fish into "not-fish" and "not-blood" with the death of his mother, and the idea that his own parent can so suddenly cease to exist is as traumatic for him as it is for Darl.

The various characters' interior monologues often seem detached from the rest of the novel, but there is in fact a very careful structure holding them all in place. One particularly noteworthy example of this structure can be found in the overlapping, but still contradictory, passages in which Dewey Dell and Vardaman are both in the barn. We see Dewey Dell pass by Vardaman twice, first in his account of the episode, then in hers. The two narratives are connected by the unmilked cow, a seemingly superfluous entity that reminds us that these two voices, although separated by chapters, are in fact speaking at the same time. Tellingly, Dewey Dell and Vardaman take away quite different impressions of the same experience—she thinks he has been spying on her, while he thinks she knows about his treatment of Peabody's team—but these differing perspectives are nonetheless borne out of the same urge to protect their own innocence. The storm serves a similar function, appearing in the thoughts of both Tull and Darl and providing a sort of narrative umbrella to expose the thematic link between the two men's thoughts.

SECTIONS 20–28

From Addie's funeral to Anse's complaint

> "Why?" Darl said. "If pa is your pa, why does your
> ma have to be a horse just because Jewel's is?"
>
> (See QUOTATIONS, p. 50)

TULL

Tull returns to the Bundren household with Peabody's team at ten the next morning. He discusses the high level of the river with two local farmers, Quick and Armstid. Anse comes to the door and greets them. The women go into the house while the men talk on the porch. Tull goes behind the house, where Cash is plugging up the holes Vardaman made in the coffin. The family has laid Addie into the coffin backward to accommodate the flared bottom of her wedding dress, with her feet in place at the head end, and there is a mosquito net over her face to mask the drilled holes.

Whitfield, the minister, arrives to perform the funeral as Tull is about to leave, and announces that the bridge has been washed away. The group discusses Addie's desire to be buried in Jefferson, and notes Anse's dedication to getting her body there. Cash and Tull talk about how Cash broke his leg falling from the top of a church

on which he was working. Inside, the women begin to sing, and Whitfield starts the service. The men stay outside on the porch throughout the service. As they leave, Cora is still singing. On the way home, she and Tull see Vardaman fishing in a bog. When Tull tells him there are no fish in the bog, Vardaman insists that Dewey Dell has seen one.

DARL

An accident has caused Darl and Jewel to be delayed for a few days, and as they approach the house, Darl sardonically reassures Jewel that the buzzards flying overhead do not mean that Jewel's horse is dead. Jewel curses Darl furiously, and Darl reflects that although he cannot be upset by his mother's death, as she no longer exists, Jewel's mother is a horse.

CASH

In a short burst of dialogue that is not actually credited to either speaker, Cash tries to explain to Jewel why the coffin will not balance, while Jewel curses at him to pick up the coffin regardless.

DARL

Anse, Cash, Darl, and Jewel lift the coffin and carry it out of the house, while Jewel curses them all. Cash reiterates his reservation about the coffin being unbalanced, but Jewel continues to push forward, leaving Cash to hobble after the rest of the group. Jewel almost single-handedly muscles the coffin into the wagon bed, and then curses again out loud.

VARDAMAN

Vardaman is preparing to go to Jefferson with the rest of the family. Jewel heads for the barn, and when Anse calls after him, Jewel does not respond. After Darl states that Jewel's mother is a horse, Vardaman wonders if that means his mother is a horse too, but Darl assures him otherwise. Cash brings his toolbox so he can work on Tull's place on the way back, which Anse says is disrespectful. Anse becomes even more indignant when Dewey Dell brings a package of Mrs. Tull's cakes to deliver to town.

DARL

Darl is standing with Anse when Jewel passes them, heading for the barn. Anse remarks to Darl that Jewel is disrespectful for not coming with them to bury the body. Cash proposes that they leave Jewel behind. Darl says that Jewel will catch up to them, and he sets out with the rest of the family in the wagon, which bears the coffin.

ANSE

Anse frets that Jewel lacks respect, even for his dead mother, and Darl begins to laugh in response. The wagon has just passed Tull's lane, and, just as Darl has predicted, Jewel approaches swiftly behind them on the back of his horse.

DARL

Darl sees Jewel approaching. The group passes Tull, who waves at them. Cash notes that the corpse will begin to smell in a few days, and that the coffin is still unbalanced. Darl proposes that Cash mention these observations to Jewel. A mile later, Jewel passes the wagon without acknowledgment. As Jewel passes them, his horse's hooves kick up a spot of mud on the coffin, which Cash diligently scours off.

ANSE

Anse reflects on how unfair the life of the farmer is, and reflects on the reward he expects in heaven. The family drives all day and reaches the farm of a man named Samson just before dark, only to find that torrential rains have caused the rivers to swell and flood the bridges. Anse takes comfort in the fact that he will be getting a new set of teeth.

ANALYSIS

The Bundren children show their grief in quite disparate ways, but these reactions can be broken into two rudimentary categories: physical and mental. Darl lives entirely in the realm of the mind, and almost never expresses emotion. He is so bent on rationalizing events that he refuses to acknowledge that his mother even exists anymore. Dewey Dell finds herself similarly lost in thought, although she appears to place the loss of her mother completely second to her own fears and sexual longings. In fact, for Dewey Dell, the possibility that a life is lurking inside her is more frightening than the idea of death. Cash, on the other hand, lives in a world that is entirely physical. He copes with, or ignores, the death of his mother by absorbing himself in the construction of her coffin. This fixation with building does not stop when the coffin is finished, and we see Cash fretting over the imbalance of the coffin and bringing his toolbox to the funeral. Cash's manner throughout the turmoil of Addie's death is incredibly deliberate, and it seems fitting that he acquires a limp, the perfect physical complement to his slow, stunted approach to all things emotional.

Vardaman and Jewel, however, come close to finding a middle ground between these extremes. Jewel's reaction to Addie's death is highly emotional. He almost single-handedly muscles the coffin into the wagon, and loudly curses his various siblings—actions that indicate a very strong physical and mental reaction. Moreover, Jewel displays great determination in refusing to ride with his family and in the speed with which he rushes by the rest of the Bundrens on his horse. Darl's equation of Jewel's mother with a horse certainly parallels the thinking of Vardaman, who tries to cope with the complexities of what his mother's death means to him. Vardaman's reactions are largely mental efforts, but his earlier beating of Peabody's horses, and the fact that he returns to the bog to catch another fish, demonstrate that he too reacts to things on a physical level. If the siblings' reactions do find common ground, it is because each singles out one object or issue through which to filter Addie's death: Darl with questions of existence, Jewel with horses, Vardaman with fish, Cash with his carpentry, and Dewey Dell with her sexuality.

The Bundrens' tendency to translate Addie's death into a different preoccupation reflects the work of the Austrian psychologist Sigmund Freud and his theory of sublimation. At the end of the 1920s, as Faulkner composed *As I Lay Dying*, Freud's ideas about the subconscious anxieties of man were becoming quite popular. One of Freud's most pivotal theories is that a great deal of the psyche is unconscious, and that much of what goes on in the human mind cannot be accessed simply by thinking about it. According to Freud, a severe emotional trauma, such as the death of a loved one, affects the unconscious part of one's mind in ways that are not immediately apparent to the conscious part. Equally relevant to interpreting *As I Lay Dying* is Freud's theory of sublimation, which he described as the process by which frustrated sexual energies are transformed into more socially acceptable behaviors. Though the Bundrens, with the exception of Dewey Dell, are not trying to cope with sexuality, they are trying to cope with their grief, and they deal with it by voicing strong opinions on other matters—a clear example of sublimation.

SECTIONS 29–33

From the night at Samson's to the bridge-crossing

SAMSON

On a farmstead some distance away from the Bundren household, Samson is sitting on his porch with two friends, MacCallum and Quick, when he sees the Bundrens pass by. Quick catches up to them to inform them that the bridge has washed away. The Bundrens return to Samson's, and Samson offers to put them up for the evening. The Bundrens accept, but refuse an offer of supper and sleep in the barn. Samson's wife, Rachel, considers it an "outrage" that the Bundrens are dragging Addie's coffin through the countryside and tearfully berates Samson. In the morning, Samson purposefully stays in bed until the Bundrens have gone on.

DEWEY DELL

As the family turns back to find a new way of crossing the river, Dewey Dell thinks of her dead mother and of her relationships with the men in her family. She recalls a nightmare she had when she used to share a bed with Vardaman. In the nightmare, she was neither able to see nor to feel, then she suddenly felt an unidentified "them" beneath her, "like a piece of cool silk dragged across my legs." Instead of turning into the town of New Hope, the family goes back past Tull's lane again, and again Tull waves at the passing Bundrens.

TULL

Tull takes his mule out to follow the wagon, and catches up with it down by the levee. The Bundrens stand at the river's edge, staring at the washed-out bridge and contemplating a crossing. Tull feels them all looking at him with varying degrees of hostility: Dewey Dell as if Tull had tried to touch her, Darl with his curious coolness, Cash with the appraising eyes of a carpenter, and Jewel with an overt glare. Jewel lashes out at Tull for following them down to the river, but Cash hushes him, and says some of them should use the bridge to wade across while the others drive the wagon through the shallower part of the river. Tull refuses to let them use his mule, and though both Jewel and Darl reproach him for it, Tull stands by this decision.

DARL

Darl sees Jewel glare at Tull. Darl recalls a time during Jewel's teen-age years when Jewel began falling asleep regularly during the day. He remembers how Addie used to cover up Jewel's mistakes, and how his siblings quietly took over his chores. Initially, Cash and Darl suspected that Jewel was spending his nights with a married woman. One night, Cash trailed Jewel on his midnight run, but refused to reveal Jewel's secret. A few months later, when Jewel came home on a new horse that he had purchased from Quick, it was revealed that he had been spending his nights clearing land by the light of a lantern in order to get the money. Anse became angry with Jewel, but Jewel countered that his horse would not eat a single grain of Anse's food. Later that night, Darl remembers, he found Addie crying beside Jewel, who was asleep in bed.

TULL

Tull accompanies Anse, Dewey Dell, and Vardaman on a treacher-ous crossing of the sunken bridge. They get to the other side, with Tull holding on to Vardaman's hand to make sure he gets across safely. Once they are across, Anse explains to Tull that he is trying to fulfill Addie's promise. They go to meet the wagon, which is cross-ing farther down the river.

ANALYSIS

This section uses gestures, particularly looks, to chronicle the inter-actions between the different characters. The most obvious example occurs with Tull's arrival at the river's edge, where he finds himself being stared at in very different ways by the various Bundren chil-dren. In these stares, we find a confirmation of the character traits we have seen before, and it is interesting that Tull should see sexual resentment in Dewey Dell's eyes. Clearly, Dewey Dell's suspicions are, to a certain extent, groundless, as Tull never even mentions her appearance, let alone any sexual desire for her. Dewey Dell's fixa-tion with sex, however, may come not only from her experience with Lafe or her fierce reliance on Peabody, but also from her stifling existence as the sole woman in an all-male family after Addie's death. Dewey Dell's dream as she lies next to Vardaman certainly demonstrates a sense of repression, as she finds herself unable to see or feel, but then gives way to an explosive sexuality as she finds an unnamed tangle of men beneath her. There is no real indication that the Bundren household is incestuous, and Dewey Dell's "they" might well be Lafe and Peabody, but this episode, and her glaring at Tull, certainly indicate that Dewey Dell cannot help but feel sexuality all around her.

Jewel's character is likewise further revealed, and his fierce independence confirmed, through his stare. We see Jewel rant earlier in the novel about the interference of the Tull women, but his rants against Tull show how strongly he believes that Addie's death is a private affair. This autonomy is called into question when it appears necessary for the family to use Tull's mule to cross the river. But Jewel transforms this apparent need to depend on Tull into an act of independence, as he offers to buy the beast on the spot. Tull's observes that Jewel's eyes "look like pieces of a broken plate" as he offers to buy the mule, and this angry glare is as indicative of Jewel's torn and grieving state as it is of his hatred for Tull.

Darl, on the other hand, is enigmatic, and his gaze supports this air of mystery. Dewey Dell, so good at spotting sexual desire in everyone else's eyes, feels threatened by Darl because his stare is completely lacking in lust, and she cannot understand him. She remarks that "the land runs out of Darl's eyes," suggesting that Darl has an overarching power to observe, process, and explain the environment around him. As Tull arrives at the river's edge to help the Bundrens with the crossing, he too is paralyzed by Darl. Tull remarks that the intensity of Darl's gaze makes it seem "[l]ike somehow you was looking at yourself and your doings outen his eyes." In this fictional world, where characters are wrapped up in their own thoughts and communicate very little with each other, Darl's ability to look inside others' hearts is perceived as a powerful threat. Each character treasures his or her secrets and hidden desires, and is troubled by, and resentful of, this glance that seems to lay them all bare.

SECTIONS 34–39

The river-crossing

DARL

Darl and Cash take the wagon along the river to the ford, with Jewel accompanying them on horseback. The trees break, and they spot Tull with Anse, Dewey Dell, and Vardaman on the other side of the river. The brothers argue about how they should cross. Finally, they come to an agreement. Jewel crosses upstream on horseback with a support rope, while Cash takes control of the wagon, with Darl inside. As they enter the ford, a log comes rushing at them, upsetting their progress. On Cash's advice, Darl jumps from the wagon downstream. Jewel struggles with his horse while Cash clutches at the coffin and his tools. Anse's mules float up out of the water, drowned.

VARDAMAN
Vardaman, watching from the opposite shore, sees Cash lose his grip on the coffin. Vardaman begins running along the bank, yelling at Darl to catch the coffin before it floats away. Vardaman runs past Tull, who hesitates to jump in, and rushes into the water to help Darl. Darl dodges the mules to grab hold of the coffin and struggles with it beneath the surface. When he comes up out of the water, his hands are empty. Vardaman rushes back to the bank and runs farther downstream.

TULL
Tull sees the log upset the progress of the wagon, and watches the chaos that ensues. Vardaman runs past him. Tull chastises Anse for the whole situation. Tull sees Jewel keeping hold of the coffin and the wagon by gripping a rope tied to them. Cash grabs a horse and is pulled to shore.

DARL
Darl sees Cash washed up on the riverside, unconscious, lying with a pool of vomit beside him. The other men are pulling the wreckage of the wagon out of the river. Tull ties a rope between himself and a tree to avoid being swept away by the current as he searches for things that have fallen out of the wagon. Tull asks Vardaman to keep the rope steady while he ventures into the water. Jewel is diving into the water in an effort to gather Cash's scattered tools. With several of the tools in hand, the men hover over Cash, who opens his eyes. Unable to speak, he turns his head and vomits again. Dewey Dell squats over him and calls his name. Jewel and Tull return to the river to search for Cash's saw set.

CASH
Cash remembers how he told the other family members that the coffin was not balanced, and how they should balance it.

CORA

Cora remembers a discussion she had with Addie about religion in which she criticized Addie for presuming to judge what is right and what is wrong, rather than leaving such judgment to God. Cora realizes that Addie was proud and vain, more driven by her love for the thankless Jewel than by her love for God. She remembers Addie speaking of Jewel in terms more appropriate to discussions of God, saying, "He is my cross and he will be my salvation."

ANALYSIS

In these sections, verb tenses fluctuate as each character tells his or her version of the river-crossing in either the present or the past tense. One of the functions of this technique is to separate the immediacy of the Bundrens' involvement with their plight from the detachment that Cora and Tull experience as observers who are not particularly invested in the Bundrens' problems. While the Bundrens generally narrate in the present tense, Cora and Vernon Tull usually give their monologues in the past tense. The past tense gives Cora and Tull an air of careful consideration, as if they have had some time to consider and evaluate the entire story before telling it with calmness, rationality, and balance. The Bundrens, on the other hand, do not have the luxury of reflection, as they are trapped in a frenzied and confusing world that allows time only for frantic explanations.

After the bridges wash out and their crossing is foiled, the Bundrens begin to seem more and more like the victims of some cosmic hex. Cash suffers the most in the failed crossing, reinjuring the leg that he first broke after falling off of a church. This injury can be seen as the result of his heroic self-sacrifice in telling Darl to leave the wagon for safety while refusing to do so himself, or it can be read as darkly comic bad luck brought on by forces outside of the Bundrens' control.

Darl's language, on the other hand, suggests something less humorous and more apocalyptic. When Darl describes the desolate air that surrounds the wagon as it enters the river, which he compares to "the place where the motion of the wasted world accelerates just before the final precipice," he employs particularly fatalistic language. Cast in this light, the river becomes a final frontier separating the Bundrens from the next life, and given the circumstances that lead up to this journey, it is hard to gauge whether Addie is being sent off to heaven or to hell.

The crossing of the river is especially fraught with religious references, and in some ways seems like the fulfillment of a long-standing curse of biblical proportions. Cora has already speculated that Vardaman's strange behavior is a curse on Addie and Anse, and she reiterates this point here, calling Addie overly proud and an idolater, due to Addie's worship of Jewel. Now the absurd circumstances of the first few sections appear to add up to a colossal punishment for these past sins. This river episode also invokes classical mythology, most notably the legend of the River Styx. According to the ancient Greeks, the River Styx flowed nine times around the underworld, a spiral of poisonous waters that were thought to dissolve any mortal vessel that attempted to make a crossing—a consequence similar to the disastrous effect that crossing the river has on the Bundrens' mule team and wagon. In classical mythology, however, the damned crossing the river were aided by a boatman named Charon, while the Bundrens have no such assistance, and are left to navigate the river alone.

SECTIONS 40–45

From Addie's monologue to the drugstore

> *That was when I learned that words are no good; that words dont ever fit even what they are trying to say at.*
> (See QUOTATIONS, p. 51)

ADDIE

The next monologue is Addie's, although it is not made explicitly clear whether her thoughts are from the coffin, or whether the narrative leaps back in time to when Addie is still living. Addie remembers working as a schoolteacher before her marriage, taking pleasure in whipping her pupils when they misbehaved. Addie then recounts Anse's terse courtship and their marriage. She says that when she gave birth to their eldest children, Cash and Darl, she felt as if her aloneness had been violated. She had declared Anse dead to her and bemoaned the uselessness of words. She recalls the extramarital passion she shared, and then lost, with Whitfield, the minister. As a result of that brief affair, Addie became disillusioned by that fact that someone supposedly virtuous could engage in such sinful behavior. She eventually gave birth to Jewel, Whitfield's bastard son. Addie remembers giving birth to Dewey Dell and Vardaman, and describes the births as the final payments in an emotional debt to Anse, after which she was free to die. Addie recalls some of Cora's remarks about sin and salvation, and dismisses them as empty words.

WHITFIELD

Whitfield overcomes temptation, and resolves to go to the Bundren household and confess his affair with Addie to Anse before Addie can do so herself. Although the bridge is washed away, Whitfield is able to cross. Upon reaching Tull's house, he learns that Addie is already dead, and nobody seems to know about the affair. Whitfield decides that this turn of events must be a sign from God. He pays his last respects, and leaves without confessing.

DARL

Darl helps lay the semiconscious Cash on top of the coffin. Jewel rides ahead to get Armstid's team, and the Bundrens ride up to the Armstid household. They carry Cash inside. Armstid offers the house to the Bundrens for the evening, but Anse declines and the Bundrens return to the shed. After initially refusing Armstid's offer of supper, Anse accepts. Jewel remains behind to attend to the horses.

ARMSTID

Over supper, Armstid and Anse discuss the purchase of a new team of mules. Armstid offers Anse the use of his team, but Anse declines. Jewel rides out to find Peabody, but returns with a horse doctor instead, who sets Cash's broken leg. Cash faints from the pain but does not complain. The next morning, Anse rides off on Jewel's horse to see about purchasing a team. Armstid watches Vardaman fight off a slew of buzzards that have gathered around Addie's coffin. Jewel attempts to move the wagon out of the shed, but Darl refuses to help. Late in the day, Anse returns to announce that he has purchased a team. He explains that he has mortgaged his farm equipment, used some money that Cash was saving to buy a gramophone, used some money from his own false teeth fund, and traded away Jewel's horse. After the first shock wears away, Jewel rides off on his horse. Without the horse, it looks as if the trade will not go through. However, the next morning, a farmhand comes by with a team of mules, saying that the horse was left, unattended, on the land of the man who made the trade with Anse.

VARDAMAN
Vardaman is traveling with his family in the wagon, and watches a group of buzzards circling above them in the sky.

MOSELEY
Moseley, a shopkeeper in the town of Mottson, sees a young woman browsing in his store, and asks her if she needs assistance. Moseley is shocked when the young woman, Dewey Dell, hints that she is in search of an abortion treatment. He flatly refuses to provide her with one, saying that he is a churchgoing man. The young woman insists, and tells Moseley that Lafe told her the drugstore would give her the proper treatment for ten dollars. Moseley still refuses, and advises the young woman to marry her precious Lafe. After the young woman leaves, Moseley hears more about the Bundren family from his assistant. The assistant tells Moseley that Anse had an encounter with the Mottson marshal earlier about the stench of Addie's eight-day-old corpse. One of the sons was seen buying cement to set his brother's leg, and then the family left Mottson.

ANALYSIS
The sudden introduction of Addie's voice into the narrative is puzzling, and, like Darl's uncanny ability early in the novel to know what is happening at home even though he is nowhere nearby, Addie's monologue defies logical explanation. It is, however, quite well placed, and provides us with more perspective on the characters. Addie's description of Anse as a disheveled bachelor, and of their courtship as brief and matter-of-fact, accounts for his seeming lack of concern for Addie's death and his various failures as a father. Once we learn that Jewel is an illegitimate son, the mystery behind Addie's intense attachment to him is solved. For all the value we place on Addie's commentary, however, she herself has little faith in words, and understands their limits. After giving birth to Cash, she expresses her disillusionment by proclaiming that "[w]ords were no good." The words "marriage" and "motherhood" have been robbed of their expressiveness, and no longer have anything to do with Addie's experience. Just as linguistic representations of the abstract concepts of marriage and motherhood have become meaningless for Addie, so have the actual institutions been stripped of their positive qualities.

Addie's disillusionment with religion points to a deeper preoccupation in the novel with the extent to which religion, sin, and morality determine the actions of the characters. Although these elements factor heavily into the events of the novel, Faulkner is rarely moralistic or judgmental: although some characters know what is right and wrong, they often feel free to disregard that awareness, while other characters, such as Addie, are confused about what is morally correct in the first place.

Addie's spiritual crisis stands in stark contrast with that of Whitfield, whose spiritual integrity remains untarnished in spite of all his failings. Whitfield's strong and pronounced resolution to confess all to Anse dissipates as soon as Whitfield learns of Addie's death, and he lamely justifies himself by claiming that God will accept his intention to confess in place of the actual confession. This weakness, however, does not cost Whitfield any of his esteem, and Faulkner shows a rather undisguised contempt for the clergy in this passage. Perhaps the greatest irony occurs with Cora's condemnation of Addie for her pride and her statement that not even Whitfield's prayers can save Addie from her vanity. Soon after the words are out of Cora's mouth, however, we learn about the affair, and Whitfield's whole character is unveiled to us as a sham. In fact, Whitfield's spiritual hypocrisy is similar to Anse's shameless exploitation of religious faith to justify his own interests. Whitfield, however, retains the admiration of the community, whereas Anse seems to be more or less despised. The contrast between the difficulty that the Bundrens face in crossing the river and Whitfield's relatively easy passage to apparent absolution strongly hints that divine justice is unfair.

SECTIONS 46–52

From the arrival at the Gillespie farm to the arrival in Jefferson

DARL

After the wagon stops in front of a house, Darl suggests to Dewey Dell that she go up to the door and ask to borrow a bucket for water. Cash is slowly bleeding to death. Darl takes the bucket that Dewey Dell acquires and begins mixing up cement for a cast for Cash's leg. Cash says he can last another day without it, but they go ahead and pour the cement into the splints anyway. At that moment, Jewel arrives at the wagon, and without a word climbs in. Anse tells his children that with a hill approaching they will have to get out of the wagon and ascend on foot.

VARDAMAN

Vardaman is walking up the hill with Darl, Dewey Dell, and Jewel. Vardaman is still thinking about the buzzards. He wonders where they go after sundown. He resolves to search for them that night once the family has made camp at a nearby farm.

DARL

At the farm that evening, Darl helps set the coffin against an apple tree. Because of the heat, Cash complains of pain in his leg, which has begun to swell. They pour some water over it. Darl repeatedly asks Jewel who his father was, but Jewel refuses to answer.

VARDAMAN

Vardaman and Darl go out by moonlight to the apple tree where the coffin rests. Darl tells Vardaman that they can hear Addie speaking to them, and Vardaman puts his ear to the coffin. They return to the barn to check on Cash. Later, as Dewey Dell and Vardaman prepare to go to sleep on the back porch, Anse, Darl, Jewel, and the Gillespie boy, the son of the farmer who is hosting the Bundrens, all move the coffin from under the apple tree to the barn. Vardaman goes in search of the buzzards, and witnesses Darl setting fire to the barn. He tells Dewey Dell his secret, and she tells him not to say anything about it to anyone.

DARL

Darl runs with Jewel down to the barn, which is ablaze. The others emerge from the house to witness the spectacle. Jewel enters the inferno, making a furious attempt to free the horses and mules from the burning barn. He then risks his life to save the coffin.

VARDAMAN

Vardaman looks at the burned remains of the barn. The coffin is carried back to the apple tree. The family goes inside to attend to Cash, whose foot and leg have turned black as a result of the confining cast. Anse makes an amateur attempt to break off the cement cast. Jewel's back goes red from burns sustained in the fire, then black from the medicine that Dewey Dell gives him. Darl remains outside by the apple tree, lying on top of the coffin and weeping.

DARL

From the shops and signs that the wagon is now passing, Darl deduces that the family is approaching Jefferson. Cash is resting on top of the coffin, and Anse decides that they must get him to a doctor. Suddenly, Dewey Dell declares that she needs to head for the bushes. When she returns, she has changed into her Sunday dress. The wagon passes a group of pedestrians, who remark on the odor of the corpse. Jewel angrily confronts one of them, who pulls out a knife. Without admitting his brother is wrong, Darl restrains Jewel and settles the dispute, and they drive on into Jefferson.

ANALYSIS

Over time, most of the Bundren narrators become more rational in their recounting of events. Vardaman's initial frantic outbursts cool into an absorbed perceptiveness more representative of his character. Dewey Dell's hysteria gives way to a more practical outlook, and Cash progresses from a reticent carpenter into the most even-keeled and reflective voice of all. But Darl, who starts out as the clearest narrator, gradually adopts a style that reflects blind passion and anger. The literary term for this kind of inversion is *chiasmus,* or the diagonal or crosswise arrangement of elements. The term "chiasmus" comes from "chi," the Greek word for the letter "X" in the Greek alphabet. The letter "X" represents the simplest form of chiasmus, as the second stroke forming the letter is a perfect inversion of the first stroke. In *As I Lay Dying,* the most chiastic element is the inversion of the characters' attitudes after Addie's death. Whereas Darl's brothers and sister climb out of an initial period of grief into an acceptance of their loss, Darl himself falls into despair. In *As I Lay Dying,* the use of chiasmus serves the vital purpose of giving form to a story that might otherwise fail to have a narrative arc. The thoughts and words of the narrators may be jumbled, but the novel itself is not—it focuses on and finds order in the emotions of its protagonists, rather than in the events that drive these emotions.

Darl's burning of the barn and the changes in his narrative ability are symptoms of deeper changes in his character. Darl's questioning of Jewel's paternity reveals the same cruel streak that he displays when they first learn of Addie's death and Darl sardonically reassures Jewel that Jewel's horse is not dead. When he rescues Jewel from a brawl with a knife-wielding townsman, however, Darl reveals his concern with both his brother's safety and dignity. This last action suggests that Darl, even though he burns down a barn—an especially serious crime in the agricultural South of Faulkner's time, when barns were a key part of industry and personal survival—is moving toward a reconciliation with the living members of his family. Even Darl's unkind words about Jewel's father may be a symptom of this reconciliation, as Darl tries to deal honestly with yet another issue haunting the family.

With all the dysfunction plaguing the Bundrens, however, it is no surprise that Darl's attempt to deal honestly with issues proves to be destructive. The members of the Bundren family have very little to their name in the way of either possessions or dignity. Because they have little else in their lives with which to preoccupy themselves, they adhere inflexibly to their mission to bury Addie in Jefferson. This gesture, however, costs them what little of value they do have: Anse's mules, Jewel's horse, and Cash's leg, the loss of which amounts to the loss of his livelihood. The novel frequently mentions the stench of both Cash's rotting leg and Addie's corpse to remind us of the family's desperate situation. In burning the barn, Darl may be seeking to stop this cycle of putridity. The barn's flames complete the image of the family stuck in an inferno, but this kind of catharsis is needed to shake the family out of its stupor. Whether or not it succeeds, however, is up for debate. Darl's burning of the barn does hasten reconciliation between Darl and Jewel, but it also compounds the family's woes, and the mission to bury Addie is no closer to completion than before.

SECTIONS 53–59

From Darl's departure to Anse's marriage

> [A]int none of us pure crazy and aint none of us pure
> sane. . . . [I]t aint so much what a fellow does, but it's
> the way the majority of folks is looking at him when
> he does it. (See QUOTATIONS, p. 52)

CASH

Cash explains why the family has decided to send Darl to a mental institution in Jackson. He says that because Gillespie was prepared to sue the Bundrens over the fire, they had no other choice. The family drives into Jefferson. Darl proposes that they treat Cash's leg before burying Addie. Cash says that he can wait. Anse stops the wagon in front of a house and enters to ask for a shovel. A gramophone is playing inside, which interests Cash. Anse stays longer than expected and eventually emerges with two shovels. After the Bundrens finish burying Addie, the men from the institution show up to take Darl away. Darl struggles violently, but his family, with Dewey Dell in the lead, helps to subdue him. Darl sits on the ground, stunned, laughing uncontrollably.

PEABODY

Peabody treats Cash's broken leg. He says that Cash will hobble on a shortened leg for the rest of his life—if he walks again. Peabody berates Cash for allowing Anse to set his leg in cement and loudly deplores Anse's treatment of his children.

MACGOWAN

MacGowan, a clerk at the Jefferson drugstore, is at work when a young girl enters. MacGowan finds the young woman, Dewey Dell, attractive, and he takes advantage of the the absence of his boss by pretending to be a doctor. Dewey Dell explains her situation to MacGowan, who understands that she wants an abortion. She offers him ten dollars to perform the operation. MacGowan's cover is almost blown when a coworker interrupts them, but he lies his way out of it. He tells Dewey Dell that ten dollars is not enough, and asks her how far she is willing to go for this operation. Desperate, the young woman agrees. MacGowan picks a bottle at random for her to drink and tells her to meet him back at the store that night for the rest of the procedure. She drinks from the bottle and leaves. That night, MacGowan closes the store down and waits there. Dewey Dell arrives promptly with a young boy, Vardaman, who waits on the curb outside the store. MacGowan hands Dewey Dell a box of talcum capsules and tells her to come to the cellar with him.

VARDAMAN

Vardaman accompanies Dewey Dell on an evening walk through Jefferson. They pass through the dark streets and the closed stores. Vardaman wants to stop to look at a toy train, but Dewey Dell takes them in the other direction, where she enters a drugstore, leaving Vardaman on the curb. Vardaman sits alone in the town square, thinking about how Darl went crazy, and stares at a lone cow. Dewey Dell emerges, and as they walk back to their hotel, she repeatedly makes the cryptic comment that "it" will not work.

DARL

Darl rants to himself as he is brought to the mental institution by armed guards. He switches madly between the first and third person perspective as he wonders why Darl cannot stop laughing, even as he lies in a dirty, grimy cell in Jackson.

DEWEY DELL

Anse asks Dewey Dell about her ten dollars. She claims that she made it by selling Cora's cakes. Anse wants to borrow the money, but Dewey Dell explains that it is not hers to loan. She says that if he takes the money from her, he will be a thief. Anse takes the money anyway and leaves the hotel.

CASH

Cash remembers Anse going back to the house to return the spades and remaining inside for a long time. That night, a sheepish Anse goes into town to attend to some unnamed business. The next morning, as the family prepares to leave Jefferson, Anse goes out, telling his children to meet him later. They wait for him on a corner, eating bananas. Eventually Anse arrives, wearing a new set of false teeth and escorting a stern-looking woman who carries a gramophone. Looking both sheepish and proud, Anse introduces all of his children to the woman, and tells them all to "[m]eet Mrs. Bundren."

> "It's Cash and Jewel and Vardaman and Dewey Dell," pa says, kind of hangdog and proud too, with his teeth and all, even if he wouldn't look at us. "Meet Mrs Bundren," he says. (See QUOTATIONS, p. 53)

ANALYSIS

In the novel's final chapters, Cash emerges as the most objective and rational member of the family, and is consequently the most obvious choice to inherit the role of narrator from the ranting Darl. Up to this point, Cash has been the least vocal of the Bundrens, giving him a sort of neutrality in the politics of the family. This neutrality allows him to tell the final episode of the story with an impartial eye that is rare in this conflicted, self-loathing family. Cash's reflections on Darl's insanity accurately articulate the novel's skepticism about absolute moral claims. Although Cash makes no apology for the family's decision to commit Darl to a mental institution, he goes on

SUMMARY & ANALYSIS

to say that madness "aint so much what a fellow does" as how "the majority of folks is looking at him when he does it." This intellectually complex statement acknowledges the role that society plays in determining people's fates and interpretations of themselves. Cash's use of the past tense also indicates his strong rationality, as though he has fully thought out the actions he describes. We have seen similar perspectives from characters outside the Bundren family, suggesting that Cash has escaped his family's dysfunction and has arrived at some degree of normalcy.

In Darl's final narrative, the degeneration of the voice of a once insightful and rational man into that of an incomprehensible schizophrenic is shown by his use of wildly incongruous pronouns and points of view. Darl speaks of himself sometimes as "I" and sometimes as "Darl," indicating that he sees his inner, private self as an identity separate from his outer, social self. Similarly, his comment toward the end of his monologue that "Darl is our brother" indicates that he is assuming the perspective of his siblings. Through this insane raving, we can see traces of the old Darl, who earlier senses his siblings' deepest secrets. While Darl earlier has the uncanny ability to get inside others' heads, he is now somewhat locked out of his own head.

The family members' reactions to Darl's incarceration seem far less intense than their reactions to Addie's death, and they quickly return to their usual preoccupations following Darl's removal. Vardaman mentions Darl and Addie repeatedly in his final monologue, but he is also enraptured by the buzzards and by a toy train he sees in town. Cash seems resigned to Darl's being put in an asylum, and Dewey Dell neglects to mention Darl at all. Anse seems to bear no scars, nor to have learned any lessons, from the tribulations of his journey. Anse's stay in Jefferson is brief, but culminates in a second marriage that happens so quickly it is almost comic. Anse embodies the contrast between the macabre and the mirthful, between high seriousness and cheap farce, and his status is emblematic of the contradictions that permeate the narrative. These contradictions underscore the novel's key idea that there is no absolute perception of reality, and that one person's pain is another's comedy. The differing reactions to Darl's removal serve as a last reminder that even the most cataclysmic events do not set off a universal reaction, and that events are shaped entirely by the perspective and experience of the person witnessing them.

IMPORTANT QUOTATIONS EXPLAINED

1. That's what they mean by the love that passeth
   understanding: that pride, that furious desire to hide
   that abject nakedness which we bring here with
   us, . . . carry stubbornly and furiously with us into the
   earth again.

Peabody has these thoughts about the dying Addie Bundren at the end of Section 11. A seasoned doctor, Peabody approaches Addie's situation with an objective, hard-nosed realism. Here, Peabody comments on Addie's love for her favorite son, Jewel, who has refused to come to her and bid her farewell before setting out on a short trip, even though there is a good chance she will be dead when he returns. In Peabody's mind, Addie's love for Jewel is unrequited, and her determination to continue loving him with such force is a sign of stubbornness, irrationality, and pride. From our perspective, there is some irony in Peabody's statement. Peabody does not know, for example, that Jewel is the product of Addie's illicit, passionate affair with Whitfield and thus that her devotion to Jewel may not be as irrational as it seems. Additionally, Peabody says that Addie is no more than a "pack-horse" to Jewel, unaware that the living creature to which Jewel shows more devotion than any other happens to be a horse.

In making reference to the "love that passeth understanding," Peabody invokes a reference to the biblical book Ephesians, in which the same phrase is used to describe the love of Christ (Ephesians 3:19). Peabody's use of a biblical reference to describe a very human relationship demonstrates the degree to which the characters in the novel understand their experiences along religious lines. *As I Lay Dying* is not itself didactic or moralistic, and Faulkner's aim is not to suggest that God is exercising judgment upon the Bundrens. However, this passage reveals the extent to which the characters themselves consciously and unconsciously interpret their lives using the values and explanations provided by the Bible.

2.   "Jewel's mother is a horse," Darl said.
         "Then mine can be a fish, can't it, Darl?" I said.
              . . .
         "Then what is your ma, Darl?" I said.
         "I haven't got ere one," Darl said. "Because if I had
      one, it is *was*. And if it was, it cant be *is*. Can it?"

Vardaman's equation, in Section 24, of his mother's death with the
fish's death at first seems a childish, illogical connection. This asso-
ciation, however, along with Darl's linking of the question of existence to a matter of "was" versus "is," allows these two uneducated
characters to tackle the highly complex matters of death and existence. The bizarre nature of this exchange epitomizes the Bundrens'
inability to deal with Addie's death in a rational way. For Darl, language has a peculiar control over Addie's existence: he believes that
she cannot be an "*is*," or a thing that continues to exist, because
she is a "*was*," or a thing that no longer exists. For Vardaman,
objects that are similar to each other become interchangeable: he
assigns the role of his mother to the fish, for example, because the
fish is dead like Addie. These somewhat systematic responses to
Addie's death demonstrate that Darl and Vardaman, like the rest of
their family, are unable to have a healthy emotional response to
death.

3. [W]ords dont ever fit even what they are trying to say
    at. . . . [M]otherhood was invented by someone who
    had to have a word for it because the ones that had
    the children didn't care whether there was a word for
    it or not.

The novel again turns a critical eye on language in this quotation, which is drawn from Section 40, the only section in the novel narrated by Addie Bundren. Addie describes her discovery that life is miserable as a sort of trick on the part of language, which promises fulfilling things but can deliver only empty words. To speak of something, this passage infers, is far easier, and leads to far more pleasant conclusions, than to experience it. This philosophy may partially explain the laconic nature of most of the novel's characters, and their unwillingness to communicate with words, relying more heavily upon visual communication and action. One of the remarkable achievements of *As I Lay Dying*—a novel composed, of course, of nothing but words—is to show how a world in which verbal communication is ineffective or unreliable can be as rich with emotion and experience as one that is highly verbal.

QUOTATIONS

4. Sometimes I think it aint none of us pure crazy and aint none of us pure sane until the balance of us talks him that-a-way. It's like it aint so much what a fellow does, but it's the way the majority of folks is looking at him when he does it.

Cash relates these thoughts in Section 53, as he discusses his family's decision to commit his brother Darl to a mental institution after Darl burns down Gillespie's barn in an attempt to destroy Addie's corpse. Cash's conclusion—that sanity is a relative term and that Darl's apparent insanity is nothing more than his failure to conform to social norms—reflects an understanding of the radical subjectivity that the novel's various narrative perspectives create. In light of the injury, property loss, and stench that the Bundrens' attempt to bury Addie has created, Cash does appear to have a point with his suggestion that Darl is not insane. The reason that Darl, and not the rest of his family, is declared insane may be simply that the perspectives of the rest of the Bundren family outnumber his.

5.   "It's Cash and Jewel and Vardaman and Dewey Dell,"
      pa says, kind of hangdog and proud too, with his
      teeth and all, even if he wouldn't look at us. "Meet
      Mrs Bundren," he says.

This passage, also narrated by Cash, ends the novel. Anse Bundren's
children have braved fire, flood, and humiliation to deliver their
mother's corpse to the gravesite she had chosen, and now, the day
after she is buried, Anse appears sporting a set of false teeth and a
new wife. There have been a number of ironic moments in the novel
up to this point, but this last scene is the most ironic of all. As the
final moment of the novel, it casts a shadow over the entire work—
all of the events preceding it now appear either farcical or tragic.
The image of the sheepish but proud Anse standing in front of his
astonished brood with his new wife and false teeth certainly has its
comic elements, but is especially cynical in light of the fact that this
woman must certainly be the one who has loaned Anse the shovels
with which to bury Addie. That the title of "Mrs. Bundren" can pass
so easily from one woman to another makes us wonder if, in fact,
Darl isn't right to question whether any of us exist at all.

Key Facts

FULL TITLE
As I Lay Dying

AUTHOR
William Faulkner

TYPE OF WORK
Novel

GENRE
Satire of heroic narrative; rural novel; comedy; tragedy

LANGUAGE
English

TIME AND PLACE WRITTEN
1929–1930; Oxford, Mississippi

DATE OF FIRST PUBLICATION
October 6, 1930

PUBLISHER
Jonathan Cape & Harrison Smith, Inc.

NARRATOR
The narration is in the first person, though it is split between fifteen different characters

POINT OF VIEW
The point of view shifts between the fifteen different narrators, each with a unique personal interpretation and reaction to the events of the novel

TONE
Varies from narrator to narrator: tragic, comic, calm, hysterical, emotional, detached

TENSE
Mostly present, occasionally past

SETTING (TIME)
1920s

SETTING (PLACE)
A rural area in fictional Yoknapatawpha County, Mississippi

PROTAGONIST
Darl Bundren

MAJOR CONFLICT
When transporting the recently deceased Addie to her burial
site, the Bundren family struggles against the forces of nature
and injury in its river-crossing and the aftermath. The Bundrens
struggle internally as Darl begins to question the logic of
carrying Addie's body all the way to Jefferson.

RISING ACTION
As the Bundrens depart on their journey to bury Addie, they find
the bridges are washed out, forcing them to ford the river. In the
process, the team of mules is lost, and the slowness of their
journey means that Addie's corpse begins to rot.

CLIMAX
Darl burns down a barn where the family has stored Addie's
coffin for the night

FALLING ACTION
Addie is buried; Darl is apprehended by officers from a mental
asylum; Anse Bundren remarries

THEMES
The impermanence of existence and identity; the tension
between words and thoughts; the relationship between
childbearing and death

MOTIFS
Pointless acts of heroism; interior monologues; issues of
social class

SYMBOLS
Animals; Addie's coffin; tools

FORESHADOWING
Kate Tull's prediction that Anse will remarry quickly
foreshadows Anse's rapid remarriage after Addie's burial;
warnings and hesitation on the part of certain characters hint
that the river-crossing will be disastrous.

KEY FACTS

STUDY QUESTIONS & ESSAY TOPICS

STUDY QUESTIONS

1. *Do you consider* As I Lay Dying *to be primarily a comic or a tragic novel?*

Critics have approached this question from radically different perspectives. Some have argued that *As I Lay Dying* is primarily a satire of the rural poor, while others have made the case that it is a more serious portrait of psychological tensions in a family under strain. Perhaps the novel is best described as a tragicomedy, a work with elements of both tragedy and comedy mixed together. It seems fair to say that, as the narrative progresses, the elements of tragedy and comedy both intensify, and the funniest moments are also the saddest. Cash's martyrlike endurance of the pain in his leg is both upsetting and absurd, as is Anse's final, sweeping statement of selfishness when he immediately takes a new wife and spends his daughter's money on a pair of false teeth. Darl's mad laughter at the end of the novel may provide the best—and most disturbing—clue as to how the novel should be read, as he challenges us with the question, "Why do you laugh? . . . Is it because you hate the sound of laughing?"

2. *Comment on the novel's structure. What does Faulkner accomplish by choosing an unconventional narrative style?*

The multiple voices employed in telling the story give the narrative a richness that would be impossible to obtain through a single perspective. Because each character has his or her own set of moral views, the tension between these perspectives forces us to think critically about the issues at hand. Of course, Faulkner does run the risk of losing his audience by making his story so hard to follow at times. In a sense, Faulkner sacrifices psychological depth to achieve greater psychological breadth—instead of having us fully understand Darl, or Jewel, or any of the other Bundren children, we are given frequent tastes of all of them. Whether or not Faulkner's style is effective for storytelling, his innovative technique certainly influences our perceptions of the novel's content. Unsure which character's perspective to adopt regarding events, we are inclined to concentrate less on events than on the images, words, and psychological processes that circulate in the characters' minds.

3. *How does the narrative style of* As I Lay Dying *affect the reader's or the characters' perceptions of time?*

The phenomenon of time gets the same jarring, disjointed treatment as everything else in the novel, due to the fact that it too is subjective. A minute of mundane experience passes more slowly than a minute of excitement. Thus, the interior monologue of any individual can move through events with dizzying speed or excruciating slowness, and can refer to events from the past, present, and future in any order. This chronological disorderliness is not, however, limited to a jumbled conception of time within passages. The flow of time from one monologue to the next is every bit as disorderly as the flow of time within a single monologue. In each of the fifty-nine narratives in the novel, we have a different voice experiencing time in a different manner, through the lens of different hopes and concerns. Two different characters may experience the same moment in time in two completely different fashions. We, however, can process the various characters' experiences only one at a time, and, consequently, the same event is often presented several times, from different perspectives. This approach can make it difficult for us to keep track of the passage of time and the sequence of events, but it furthers the novel's goal of presenting a series of psychological portraits.

Suggested Essay Topics

1. At the end of the novel, Darl is committed to an insane asylum for setting a barn on fire. What other factors may be involved in his family's decision to commit him? What justification, if any, is there for his act of arson?

2. Provide a close reading of Addie's monologue in the middle of the novel. What do we learn about her life? How is it that a dead woman's voice can enter the narrative? Why does Faulkner introduce Addie's voice when he does?

3. With the exception of Addie, the Bundrens have probably all received very little schooling. Do their monologues demonstrate or contradict this apparent fact?

4. Compare the monologues of members of the Bundren family with those of outside observers, like Tull, Cora, and Moseley. Which set of monologues do you feel provides a more accurate perspective on events?

5. Which characters do you think are the most heroic? Which are the most unheroic? What does the story say about the ideal of heroism?

REVIEW & RESOURCES

QUIZ

1. In Cora Tull's opinion, which Bundren son loves his mother the most?

   A. Jewel
   B. Cash
   C. Vardaman
   D. Darl

2. For whom do Darl and Jewel make a delivery?

   A. Anse
   B. Peabody
   C. Tull
   D. Addie

3. Who is the father of Dewey Dell's unborn child?

   A. Vernon Tull
   B. MacGowan
   C. Lafe
   D. Whitfield

4. How did Cash break his leg the first time?

   A. Falling off a church
   B. Crossing a flooded river
   C. Accidentally hitting it with a hammer
   D. Trying to ride Jewel's horse

5. What does Vardaman think his mother is?

   A. A horse
   B. A buzzard
   C. An angel
   D. A fish

6.   What is Cash saving his money to buy?

   A.   A new saw
   B.   A gramophone
   C.   Crutches
   D.   A new horse for Jewel

7.   What was Addie's profession before she was married?

   A.   Teacher
   B.   Nurse
   C.   Cook
   D.   Undertaker

8.   From what disability does Anse Bundren suffer?

   A.   A game leg
   B.   Blindness
   C.   A speech defect
   D.   A hunchback

9.   Whose barn does Darl burn down?

   A.   Samson's
   B.   Gillespie's
   C.   Anse's
   D.   Armstid's

10.   With what object in a store window is Vardaman obsessed?

   A.   A fishing pole
   B.   Bananas
   C.   A toy train
   D.   A drug that claims to bring the dead back to life

11.   With what literary movement is Faulkner most often associated?

   A.   Social realism
   B.   Modernism
   C.   Post-modernism
   D.   Romanticism

REVIEW & RESOURCES

12. What is the name of the fictional county in which Faulkner sets a large number of his novels?

    A. Bloom
    B. Kranakapchote
    C. Yoknapatawpha
    D. Jefferson

13. What is Anse looking forward to buying when the family gets to Jefferson?

    A. A new team of mules
    B. A headstone for Addie
    C. An abortion drug for Dewey Dell
    D. A set of false teeth

14. Who builds Addie's coffin?

    A. Anse
    B. Cash
    C. Whitfield
    D. Vardaman

15. Which Bundren child is not Anse's?

    A. Jewel
    B. Cash
    C. Darl
    D. Dewey Dell

16. What is in the capsules that MacGowan prepares for Dewey Dell?

    A. Turpentine
    B. A sleeping potion
    C. Talcum powder
    D. An herb that induces abortion

17. What is the first thing Jewel saves from the fire?

    A. Cash
    B. Addie's coffin
    C. The team
    D. The family's money

18. What is Whitfield's occupation?

    A. Farmer
    B. Minister
    C. Shopkeeper
    D. Doctor

19. Why does Jewel insult a man on the road as the family nears Jefferson?

    A. The man mentions the smell of Addie's corpse
    B. The man tries to steal Jewel's horse
    C. The man tries to seduce Dewey Dell
    D. The man is tailgating the Bundrens' wagon

20. How does Cash make it to shore after the accident?

    A. Darl rescues him
    B. Jewel rescues him
    C. A horse pulls him to shore
    D. He gets caught in some bushes

21. Why does Cash's leg turn black?

    A. His cast is poorly made
    B. He gets burned in the fire
    C. He gets bitten by a snake
    D. He reacts to the medicine Dewey Dell gives him

22. Why does Vardaman drill holes in his mother's coffin?

    A. He wants to get her out
    B. He wants to see her
    C. He wants her to be able to breathe
    D. He wants to hurt her

23. Which of the following does Anse not use to buy a new team?

    A. Money from the sale of Jewel's horse
    B. Money from his own false teeth fund
    C. Money from Cash's savings
    D. Money from Darl's savings

24. Who helps the Bundrens pull wreckage from the river?

   A.   Samson
   B.   Tull
   C.   Armstid
   D.   Gillespie

25. About whom does Addie say, "He is my cross and he will be my salvation"?

   A.   Anse
   B.   Jewel
   C.   Darl
   D.   Whitfield

ANSWER KEY:
1: D; 2: C; 3: C; 4: A; 5: D; 6: B; 7: A; 8: D; 9: B; 10: C; 11: B; 12: C; 13: D; 14: B; 15: A; 16: C; 17: C; 18: B; 19: A; 20: C; 21: A; 22: C; 23: D; 24: B; 25: B

Suggestions for Further Reading

BROOKS, CLEANTH. *William Faulkner: First Encounters.* New Haven, Connecticut: Yale University Press, 1983.

———. *William Faulkner: The Yoknapatawpha Country.* New Haven, Connecticut: Yale University Press, 1963.

COX, DIANNE L., ed. *William Faulkner's As I Lay Dying: A Critical Casebook.* New York: Garland, 1985.

GAY, PETER. "Sigmund Freud: A Brief Life." In *Introductory Lectures on Psychoanalysis,* by Sigmund Freud. New York: W. W. Norton and Company, 1989.

MERIWETHER, JAMES B., and MICHAEL MILLGATE, eds. *Lion in the Garden: Interviews with William Faulkner, 1926–1962.* Lincoln, Nebraska: University of Nebraska Press, 1980.

SWISHER, CLARICE, ed. *Readings on William Faulkner.* San Diego: Greenhaven Press, 1998.

VOLPE, EDMOND L. *A Reader's Guide to William Faulkner.* New York: Farrar, Straus and Giroux, 1964.

WADLINGTON, WARWICK. *As I Lay Dying: Stories out of Stories.* New York: Twayne Publishers, 1992.

WILLIAMS, DAVID. *Faulkner's Women: The Myth and the Muse.* Montreal: McGill-Queen's University Press, 1977.

SPARKNOTES STUDY GUIDES: